10/98

19.⁹³

Housing

Our Feathered Friends

Housing
Our Feathered Friends

by Dean T. Spaulding

BIRDER'S
BOOKSHELF

Lerner Publications Company • Minneapolis

To my family and friends, for putting up with my hobby for all these years.

Photo Acknowledgments

All photos copyrighted to and reproduced with the permission of: Richard Day/Daybreak Imagery, pp. 2, 6, 12, 18, 26, 30, 35, 39, 41, 51; Todd Fink/Daybreak Imagery, p. 20; Rob Curtis/ The Early Birder, pp. 8, 14, 22, 28, 48, 54; Perry J. Reynolds, pp. 11, 24, 45; Dean T. Spaulding, pp. 16, 53; Kathy Adams Clark, p. 33.

Front cover photo courtesy of Richard Day/Daybreak Imagery.
Back cover photo courtesy of Rob Curtis/The Early Birder.

Page 2: A prothonotary warbler

Library of Congress Cataloging–in–Publication Data

Spaulding, Dean T.
    Housing our feathered friends / Dean T. Spaulding
      p.   cm. — (Birder's bookshelf)
    Includes index.
    Summary: Provides information on the nests birds build and instructions for building several birdhouses at various levels of difficulty.
      ISBN 0-8225-3176-3 (alk. paper)
    1. Birdhouses — Design and construction. [1. Birdhouses — Design and construction. 2. Birds — Nests.] I. Title. II. Series: Spaulding, Dean T. Birder's bookshelf.
    QL676.5.S66 1997
    690'.892 — dc20   96-25129

Manufactured in the United States of America
1 2 3 4 5 6 – JR – 02 01 00 99 98 97

CONTENTS

A chipping sparrow's nest and three eggs

Chapter 1

Welcome Home!

February 19 is National Homes For Birds Day, a day when people can think about the importance of nesting in the lives of birds. Nesting refers to the time when birds build nests, lay eggs, and raise their young. Most birds nest in the spring and summer.

One of the best ways to help birds during nesting season is to give them plenty of safe places in which to build their nests. Some birds build nests at the base of tree branches. Other birds build nests inside protective structures, such as holes in decaying trees. Still other birds build nests inside birdhouses that people provide for them. Many birds build nests right in people's yards.

In this book, you will learn how birds build nests and raise their young. You will learn to make birdhouses out of simple materials found around your own house. By hanging up homemade birdhouses in your yard, you'll be able to see the nesting process up close. You'll even provide materials that birds can use when building their nests.

You don't really need a special day to remember the importance of bird nesting. You can build birdhouses all year-round. When birds return to your yard in spring, your homemade birdhouses will welcome them.

The ideas in this book are only the beginning. Think of your own ideas for homemade birdhouses. Hang your creations outside and see whether the birds use them. Tell a friend about your new ideas. The more houses people put up for the birds, the more birds will come to our yards and raise their families.

A red-shouldered hawk feeds its chick in the nest.

Chapter 2

Nest Building

Though not all birds use birdhouses, all birds make nests of some kind. Some people think that nests are birds' permanent homes. But birds don't live in nests year-round. Nests are temporary shelters that birds build during nesting season to hold their eggs and to keep their young safe from predators— raccoons, foxes, and other animals that eat eggs and young birds.

Just as there are many shapes and sizes of birds, there are also many shapes and sizes of birds' nests. Some nests are bowl-shaped structures made of sticks, grass, feathers, and mud. Other nests are just holes in decaying trees or in the ground. Each kind of bird builds a different kind of nest. Ornithologists, scientists who study birds, can sometimes look at a nest and tell what kind of bird built it.

To better understand the way birds nest, ornithologists have divided birds into two groups: non-cavity nesters and cavity nesters. Most birds are non-cavity nesters. They build nests out in the open—in treetops, for example. Bald eagles are non-cavity nesters. They usually build thick nests, made of sticks, in the tops of tall pine trees.

Cavity nesters, on the other hand, build their nests inside structures that protect the nest from bad weather and predators. Of the 650 species, or specific kinds, of birds that nest north of Mexico, 85 species are cavity nesters. Of these, woodpeckers are the best known. They use their sharp bills, or beaks, to chip into wood and dig nesting cavities (holes) inside decaying tree trunks. Some cavity nesters, such as house wrens and purple martins, will use human-made birdhouses as nesting cavities.

Safe Places for Nesting

Many birds nest in places that might not seem very safe. The whippoorwill, for example, makes its nest on the ground. In fact, the whippoorwill's nest is nothing more than a shallow hole in the dirt. Birds on the ground are easy targets for predators. But the whippoorwill has brown feathers that blend in with the ground. So predators can't easily see the bird. A special coloring that helps an animal blend into its surroundings is called camouflage.

Other birds, such as certain kinds of grebes, keep their nests safe from predators by building them on tiny islands, protected on all sides by water. The grebe doesn't build just its nest, though. It builds the island too—out of reeds and floating plants.

Still other birds make their nests safe by building them under-

The whippoorwill blends in well with its surroundings.

ground. Puffins make their nests in burrows, or holes in the earth, usually about three feet deep. Belted kingfishers dig deep into riverbanks with their bills and make their nests inside.

Some birds don't mind having people around and might build nests above doorways, in the trees of your yard, or inside bird-houses that you provide. But no matter where birds are nesting—

House wrens often nest inside holes in decaying trees.

whether in the woods or in your own backyard—it is important that you never bother birds' nests, birds' eggs, or young birds in the nest.

Building the Nest

The kinds of birds that might nest in your yard will build a nest in about a week. Some birds take less time, others take longer. The American robin takes 6 to 20 days to build a nest. Birds usually work on building their nests for only a few hours each day. They spend much of the rest of their time looking for food.

Many birds build their nests by gathering together natural materials such as straw, feathers, and sticks. Often, birds use mud to plaster the walls of the nest together and soft grasses to line the inside. But other materials that birds use to build their nests might surprise you.

Hummingbirds use the sticky threads of spiderwebs to hold their nests together. One species of hawk, the gabar goshawk of Africa, gathers not only spiderwebs but also live spiders during nesting season! It collects spiders (and their webs) so that it always has a fresh spiderweb lining for its nest.

Chimney swifts act a lot like their name. They fly swiftly and often nest inside unused chimneys. They use saliva, better known as spit, to hold their nests of twigs together and to fasten the nests to chimney walls. The saliva acts a lot like cement.

The American goldfinch uses the fluffy white down of the thistle plant to make the inside of its nest soft. Thistle plants don't bloom and produce down until late summer. So while other birds are busy nesting in spring, goldfinches wait a few months before beginning to build their nests.

Great crested flycatchers and titmice sometimes use snakeskin in building their nests. The skin is built into the walls of the nest and strung outside the nesting cavity. Some ornithologists think the skin is used to frighten predators. Other scientists think that snakeskin is simply good, strong nesting material.

The ruby-throated hummingbird decorates its nest with lichen, a fungus that often grows on rocks. Lichen is light green and silver—it provides natural camouflage for the nest.

The least grebe builds its nest on a tiny island.

Horned larks nest on the ground. They make cup-shaped nests and line them with soft grasses. But horned larks add something to their homes that other birds don't. Once the nest is completed, horned larks place small, flat rocks and pebbles to one side of the nest. The rocks and pebbles make a flat surface, what we might call a patio. Scientists aren't sure what the rocks are for.

If you think snakeskin, spiderwebs, and rocks are interesting nesting materials, wait until you hear about some other materials that birds have used to build their nests over the years: bones, coins, shredded dollar bills, even golf balls!

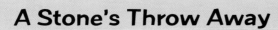

A Stone's Throw Away

By studying birds, we can learn a great deal about the natural world. In fact, studying birds' nests has actually saved human lives!

In the late 1950s, Brazil was faced with a serious health problem. Chagas' disease, transmitted by insect bites, harmed peoples' hearts and even killed some young children. The insects that carried the disease lived in cracks in dried mud.

Many poor people in Brazil lived in mud huts, which cracked in the hot sun. If huts could be made from mud that wouldn't crack, then the disease-carrying insects couldn't live in the huts, doctors reasoned.

Mario Pinotti, a Brazilian government doctor, had an idea. Pinotti remembered throwing stones at an oven-bird's nest as a boy. No matter how hard he threw the stones, the nest would not break.

After careful study, Pinotti discovered that the oven-bird built its nest with a special kind of mud, made from cow manure and sand. He led an effort to replaster thousands of poor people's huts with this special mixture. The mud didn't crack. Chagas' disease declined, and many lives were saved.

A black-crowned night-heron chick

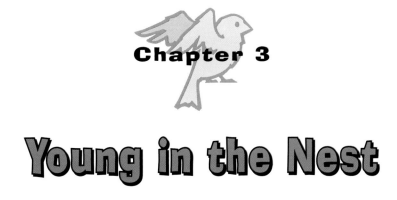

Chapter 3

Young in the Nest

Nesting season is mating season, the time when a pair of adult birds—a male and a female—mates and reproduces. The female lays the eggs. Among most species, the female lays one egg per day, until she has laid her entire clutch, or group of eggs.

Cavity nesters have large clutches of about 8 to 12 eggs. Non-cavity nesters have smaller clutches of 3 to 5 eggs. Cavity nesters have larger clutches because their eggs and young birds are better protected from predators than are the offspring of non-cavity nesters. It's easier for adult birds to feed a lot of offspring in the safety of a nesting cavity.

We can identify birds' eggs the same way we identify birds—by noting their size and color. Color on eggs acts as camouflage.

Cardinals' eggs are grayish green and covered with tiny brown spots. They blend in well with the nest and its surroundings. Predators have trouble seeing the eggs.

Birds such as woodpeckers lay pure white eggs that are easy to see. Why? Because woodpeckers are cavity nesters. Eggs inside tree cavities do not need the camouflage that eggs need on the beach, in a field, or in the grass.

For eggs to hatch, adult birds must incubate them, or keep them warm. Birds keep eggs warm by sitting on them. As adult birds incubate eggs, the young birds (called embryos) inside the eggs begin to grow.

It is usually the female bird that sits on the eggs. When the female needs to find food, the male bird might sit on the eggs in her absence. Among some species, the male brings food to the female so she doesn't have to leave the nest during incubation. If eggs are left unincubated for several hours, they might get cold, and the developing birds inside could die.

Most birds that will nest near your house have an incubation time of about two weeks. When a young bird is ready to hatch, it uses its beak to chip through the shell of its egg. This work can be very tiring for a young bird.

Many newborn birds are featherless and unable to stand, fly, or find their own food. Instead, the parents find food, such as insects and larvae, and carry it to the young birds in the nest. The group of young birds is called a brood. It is not uncommon for a pair of adult birds to raise more than one brood during nesting season. Some kinds of birds raise two or three broods per season.

Two to four weeks after hatching, the young birds are stronger. They have grown feathers and have begun to test their wings.

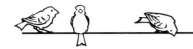

A song sparrow's nest in a blackberry bush

The young birds are then called fledglings. Adults will continue to feed and care for the fledglings for a few more weeks until they are fully able to care for themselves.

Though you should never disturb birds during nesting season, you can still enjoy watching an adult bird carry food to its nest.

Least bittern chicks in the nest

Be careful to stay more than 40 feet from the nest, however. Otherwise, you might scare the adult bird and keep it from its work. To get a good view of nesting birds without bothering them, watch them through a pair of binoculars. Binoculars are optical devices that make faraway objects look larger. They're great for viewing birds from a distance.

Keeping a Clean Nest

The most important job an adult bird has during the nesting season is to keep predators away from its nest. Camouflage is one kind of protection for birds and their eggs.

But birds keep their nests secret in other ways. Young birds of some species produce excrement, or waste, inside small white pouches called fecal sacs. Each time an adult bird brings food to the nest, it leaves carrying a fecal sac in its beak. It drops the fecal sac far away from the nest. This system helps keep the nest clean and less noticeable—by sight and smell—to predators. Members of the swallow family, including purple martins and tree swallows, drop fecal sacs over water. Predators can't possibly find the sacs and trace them back to the nest.

After young birds grow up and leave the nest, their bodies no longer produce fecal sacs to hold their excrement. (Large birds that have fewer predators, such as eagles and hawks, do not produce waste inside fecal sacs.)

Many birds protect their nests by keeping quiet. So as not to alert predators, nesting birds often slip off to gather food and return to feed their young without making the slightest peep. Because many birds are quiet when they nest, it's sometimes hard to know whether or not a bird is nesting in your yard. When studying birds, ornithologists watch for adult birds carrying fecal sacs. The sight of birds with fecal sacs tells scientists that the young birds have hatched.

Year after Year

After nesting season, many birds migrate, or travel, to warm places such as Central and South America. There, during winter months, birds find good weather and abundant food supplies.

In spring, birds migrate again, flying back to their old nesting places to raise young. A few birds reuse their old nests. Many ospreys and bald eagles repair any damage that their nests have suffered from winter weather and use the nests again in spring. Woodpeckers sometimes nest in the same holes from one year to the next. If a woodpecker abandons its hole, an American kestrel, the smallest falcon in North America, might nest there instead. Because so much work goes into digging their burrows, puffins use the same burrows year after year.

But most birds, especially those that will nest in your yard, don't reuse their nests from year to year or even from brood to brood. Most birds build a nest for one brood, then build another nest for their next.

Although a few birds reuse their nests for years, you cannot use birds' nests at all. It is against the law to collect birds' nests without a special license. If birds do build a nest in one of your birdhouses, you can remove the nest *after* nesting season—late in the fall. You can look at the nest. But you can't keep it. Only scientists who work with birds, studying their nesting habits, are permitted to keep birds' nests.

Parents must feed young birds until they are old enough to care for themselves.

Trouble Makers

Predators such as raccoons and foxes aren't the only threats to nesting birds. Even other birds can be a danger. One bird in particular preys on smaller birds—the cowbird.

Some people think that cowbirds should be called buffalo birds. In the days when wild herds of buffalo roamed the prairies of North America, cowbirds followed them,

The speckled eggs in this wood thrush's nest were laid by a cowbird.

eating insects that the herds flushed out of the prairie grasses.

Because the buffaloes were always moving around the prairies, cowbirds didn't have time to stop, build nests, and raise families in one place. Instead, cowbirds layed their eggs in the nests of birds that didn't follow the buffaloes.

Even though buffaloes no longer roam the American prairies, cowbirds still lay their eggs in other birds' nests. In a way, cowbirds use other birds as full-time babysitters. When a female cowbird finds a nest with eggs already inside it, she lays her eggs and leaves them for the other birds to hatch and raise.

Female cowbirds do more than just lay their eggs in other birds' nests, though. They also destroy some of the other birds' eggs—dropping them to the ground where they break. Since the number of eggs in the nest remains about the same, the other bird isn't likely to notice the new eggs.

Most of the time, cowbirds leave their eggs with smaller birds such as sparrows and warblers. The cowbird eggs hatch first, and the young cowbirds eat a lot more food than the smaller birds do. The cowbirds grow bigger and faster, sometimes crowding other birds right out of the nest.

Birds sometimes nest in human-made birdhouses, such as this one made from a hollow gourd.

Chapter 4

Houses for the Birds

If there were no people around, birds would use hollow trees and other natural structures as nesting cavities. Many birds do. But people also provide nesting cavities for birds. Sometimes, birds nest inside rotting wooden fence posts near roads, houses, and farms. Other times, birds nest in birdhouses that people make for them.

Here Come the Martins

Purple martins are cavity nesters. Many centuries ago, purple martins made their nests inside holes in decaying trees. Native Americans discovered that they could attract purple martins by hanging hollow gourds around the edges of their camps and settlements. Since predators would not usually venture close to human settlements, martins were happy to use the gourds as nesting cavities.

The Native Americans were also happy to have the martins in camp, since martins eat mosquitoes and other flying insects. Later, Native Americans made huge gourd "colonies" by stringing several gourds on one branch and fastening many branches together. Purple martins like to nest in large groups.

When European settlers arrived in America, they too enjoyed living near the purple martins. But instead of putting up gourds for the martins, Europeans made wooden birdhouses with many individual rooms. Because people made so many purple martin houses, purple martins lost their instinct to nest in tree cavities. They now nest only in birdhouses.

Since purple martins nest in large groups, their houses must have many rooms.

Some of your neighbors might put up special purple martin houses in spring. The houses look like apartment buildings for the birds, with separate rooms for many purple martin families. One purple martin house in Louisiana has 620 rooms!

Purple martins spend their winters in Brazil. In spring, they migrate north, returning to the same houses year after year. The oldest purple martins, called scouts, arrive early to make sure their special houses are still there. People who put up purple martin houses must have them ready when the scouts arrive in the spring.

Bluebird Trails

Bluebirds are also cavity nesters. They build their nests inside holes in decaying trees and rotting wooden fence posts. But, during the 20th century, human interference began to hurt the bluebirds. People began to cut down and remove dead trees instead of leaving them for birds to use. People replaced old wooden fence posts with plastic and metal ones.

By the 1970s, the bluebirds of North America didn't have enough places to nest. Not only had many dead trees and wooden fence posts been taken down, but birds such as house sparrows and European starlings were also competing with bluebirds for the nesting cavities that remained.

When birds don't have enough places to nest, they have a hard time raising families. Fewer birds are born each year. Because bluebirds didn't have enough nesting spots, their numbers began to decline. People worried that some species of bluebirds would die out altogether.

If the bluebird was going to survive, it would need some help.

Since people were getting rid of the bluebirds' nesting spots, people would have to provide the birds with more. That is exactly what happened.

In 1978, a group of concerned bird-watchers formed the North American Bluebird Society. Society members made hundreds of wooden nesting boxes, a special type of birdhouse. The boxes were nailed to fence posts, about 100 feet apart, to make long trails through the countryside. Some bluebird trails covered several counties.

The bluebirds began raising families in their special nesting boxes, and their numbers increased. Thanks to the work of the Bluebird Society, bluebirds have plenty of nesting spots again, and they're no longer in trouble.

Nesting boxes like this one helped the bluebird population increase.

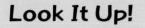

Look It Up!

Identifying birds that nest in your yard is easier if you have a field guide. Field guides are books that give pictures and descriptions of many kinds of birds. Field guides tell you each bird's size and point out unique markings. If a bird looks different from summer to winter, the field guide will show pictures for both seasons. Field guides also include maps showing where different birds live at different times of the year.

Many different field guides to birds (as well as to other animals and plants) are available in bookstores and libraries. You can even buy field guides to birds' nests and birds' eggs. Look for a field guide that applies to your region of the country. Some guides list all the birds of North America. Others describe birds in only the eastern or western part of the continent, or maybe just one state.

Bird identification involves properly matching a bird you see outdoors with a species described in your field guide. By noting a bird's size, color, and other features, you can consult your field guide and try to make a match. Identifying birds is not always easy. But with practice, you're sure to improve your skills.

Chapter 5

Birdhouse Projects

Not all birds will nest near people's homes. But many will. By building birdhouses and setting out materials that birds can use in nesting, you're likely to attract birds to your yard. Make sure your birdhouses and nesting materials are ready in early spring—just in time for nesting season.

You won't need to buy many of the materials needed for these projects. Almost all the materials are odds and ends that we already have around the house or yard—things that we often throw away after we're done using them. Let your family members know what materials you need, so they can save them for you.

The projects are divided into three difficulty levels. *Level 1* is the easiest. You don't need a parent or teacher to help you with level-1 projects. They take only about five minutes to complete, so you'll have plenty of time afterward to watch the birds nest.

A bluebird house in the
North Carolina countryside

Level-2 projects are a little more difficult. You won't need an adult with you at all times. But you might want one within yelling distance, in case you have a question with the instructions or need a helping hand. Projects from level 2 take about 15 to 30 minutes to complete. They also require more materials than do level-1 projects.

Level-3 projects are the most difficult. They take a longer time and require a lot more materials and tools than level-1 and -2 projects. Never do a level-3 project without adult help. Your whole family might want to work on level-3 projects together.

Plastic Bottle Chickadee House

If you have ever put a bird feeder filled with birdseed in your yard, you know how easy it is to attract chickadees. It's also easy to attract chickadees to a birdhouse. Chickadees are naturally curious. They are cavity nesters and will try out a birdhouse when one is made available.

Seven species of chickadees live in North America. The black-capped chickadee is the most common. No matter where you live, a species of chickadee probably nests in your area—maybe even in your yard!

Level: 1

Tools Needed:	*Materials Needed:*
scissors	2-liter green plastic soda
ruler	bottle (with cap
	attached)
	a few feet of wire

1. Wash the bottle with water and let it dry. Reattach the bottle cap.
2. Using your scissors, cut a 1½-inch-wide hole in the center of the bottle, about 6 inches from the bottom.
3. With your scissors, make a few ¼-inch slits near the top of the bottle. These slits will be airholes.
4. Wrap a piece of wire around the neck of the bottle. Make sure the wire is wrapped tight.
5. Hang the birdhouse using the wire.

Best Place to Hang the House: Hang your Plastic Bottle Chickadee House from a tree branch in a quiet corner of your yard. Pick a spot that is sunny but also gets some shade in the afternoon. A place that gets both sun and shade will help keep birds' eggs at a steady temperature.

Best Way to Clean the House: In the fall, after the birds have finished using their nest, pull the old nesting material out through the house's hole. If you can get it all out, great! Wash the house with hot, soapy water and use it again. If you can't get all the nesting material out, you might want to build a new chickadee house next year.

A Carolina chickadee

Coffee Can Wren House

Nine species of wrens live in North America. The house wren is found in most of the United States. House wrens are tiny brown birds, measuring just four inches from the tip of the beak to the end of the tail. They have small bills, which help them gather insects, and short, stubby tails that often stick straight up.

House wrens are famous for building "sloppy" nests out of sticks, twigs, and feathers. They also build nests in unusual places. People have found house wrens' nests in old boots, flowerpots, picnic baskets, tin cans, even inside the engines of cars!

Don't be surprised if a house wren in your yard doesn't stop after building one nest. Many times, the male house wren will build more than one nest. A few weeks later, the female chooses the nest she likes best. Make several Coffee Can Wren Houses and give female wrens a good selection.

Level: 1

Tools Needed:	Materials Needed:
scissors	coffee can with plastic lid
marker	a few feet of wire
quarter	

1. Place a quarter in the center of the plastic lid.
2. Trace the quarter with your marker.
3. Cut out the circle.
4. Snap the plastic lid back onto the coffee can.
5. Wrap a piece of wire around the center of the coffee can and leave 6 inches or so to use for hanging the house.

Best Place to Hang the House: Pick a spot that is partly sunny, partly shady. Don't be afraid to put your wren houses near your own house. House wrens are sociable birds. They enjoy living in people's yards and are not bothered by human activity.

If a male wren builds a nest in one of your houses but the female doesn't use it, don't remove the nest until fall. Even though the female didn't select the nest for her first brood, she might use it later in the season.

Best Way to Clean the House: The Coffee Can Wren House is easy to clean. After the young wrens have left the nest, pull the lid off the house, reach into the can, and slide the nest out. Put the nest in the trash once you are finished looking at it. Unhook the house from the wire hanger and clean it in a sink full of hot, soapy water. Return the house to the same spot and see if the wrens use it again!

Clay Pot Birdhouse

Clay flowerpots make good wren houses. Flowerpots have a small hole in the bottom for draining off excess water. A one-inch hole is all a wren needs to enter a house.

Look for an old clay pot tucked away in your basement, garage, or toolshed. Instead of looking at flowers, you can sit back, kick your feet up, and watch the birds grow!

Level: 2

Tools Needed:

wire cutters

Materials Needed:

clay pot with at least a 1-inch hole in the bottom

several feet of wire

wood putty or mud

This Carolina wren family has made its home inside a bucket.

1. Choose a tree for your birdhouse. The house won't hang from a tree branch. Instead, you'll fasten the house to the tree trunk. You must find a tree trunk that is wider than the rim of the pot.
2. Wrap a long piece of wire around the rim of the pot and place the rim against the tree trunk, about 5 feet above the ground.
3. Wrap the piece of wire around the tree trunk, fastening it again to the pot.
4. Make sure the wire is tight and the clay pot cannot shift from side to side.
5. If there are any gaps between the pot and the tree trunk, fill them with wood putty or mud.

Best Place to Put the House: Just like the Coffee Can Wren House, this house should be placed in an area that's partially shaded.

Best Way to Clean the House: In the fall, after the wrens have left, take the Clay Pot Birdhouse down and wash it with hot, soapy water. Let it dry completely before storing it for winter. No doubt, the wrens won't forget about the house. They'll be back looking for it next year.

Nesting Material Holder

You can help build a bird's nest by making a Nesting Material Holder. It's easy. You won't actually build the nest, but you'll certainly make a bird's job a little easier.

A Nesting Material Holder is a lot like a bird feeder. Instead of filling the holder with birdseed, you'll fill it with materials that birds use when building their nests. All you need are a few materials (listed on page 42) and a little creativity.

Level: 2

Tools Needed:	Materials Needed:
scissors	1/2-gallon milk carton
sharp pencil	a few feet of wire or
	string

1. Wash the milk carton with warm water. Let it dry.
2. Cut the milk carton in two and dispose of the top half.
3. With the end of your scissors, poke a hole in each side of the remaining half of the carton, near the top edge.
4. Slip a piece of wire or string through the holes and knot the ends.
5. With your pencil or the point of your scissors, make eight small holes in the bottom of the milk carton. These holes will drain any water that gets into the Nesting Material Holder. Without them, rainwater will fill the holder and ruin the materials.
6. Hang your Nesting Material Holder by the string or wire.

Best Place to Hang the Holder: Since the Nesting Material Holder has no top to keep out rain, you should hang it in a protected place. Under a porch or an overhanging roof is perfect.

Best Time to Hang the Holder: Many birds begin building their nests early in spring. So put your Nesting Material Holder out in late April. Take it down in late September.

An American robin gathers fibers for its nest.

Nesting Materials

Once you have built your Nesting Material Holder, you need to fill it. You don't have to find all the items on the following list. Two or three items are plenty.

- feathers (that have fallen from a pet or wild birds)
- horse hair (a stuffing used in old furniture)
- your own hair (The next time you get your hair cut, bring along a paper bag and take some hair home with you.)
- tree bark (Don't peel it off trees; look for bark that has already fallen to the ground.)
- straw or hay
- rope that has unraveled
- small pieces of cloth
- string
- twigs
- cotton balls (Birds that line their nests with milkweed down will appreciate cotton.)
- old shoelaces

Before putting the materials in your Nesting Material Holder, take the following steps to make sure the materials are clean and safe for the birds:

1. Place materials in a sink.
2. Run warm water over them from the tap.
3. Squeeze out excess water from the materials.
4. Place the materials on a towel.

5. With another towel, pat the materials dry.
6. Leave materials in a warm, dry place overnight.
7. Cut any long pieces (of string, for instance) into 1-inch pieces. Short pieces are safest for the birds since they're not likely to get tangled in birds' beaks or around the necks of young birds in the nest.
8. Put the materials in your Nesting Material Holder.

Check your Nesting Material Holder at least once a week. If one of the materials runs low, gather some more and add it to the rest. If you think of new items that might make good nesting materials, add those to your holder and see if the birds use them.

Observation Activity

It's interesting to watch birds take nesting materials in their beaks and fly off to their nests. When you clean out your birdhouses and remove the nests in fall, look for nesting materials that you put out for the birds yourself.

The nests will be worn from use. Spotting different materials used to build the nests might be hard. Make sure to include some colorful materials in your holder that will stand out in the nest. I always put pieces of red cloth or red yarn in my Nesting Material Holder. Then I look for red materials when I clean out my birdhouses.

Phoebe Nesting Shelf

When people think about a birdhouse, they sometimes picture a tiny house with a roof, four walls, a floor, and a hole for birds to enter and exit. But some birds won't nest in that kind of birdhouse. Phoebes, barn swallows, and robins, for instance, prefer a house with only three walls and a floor. This type of birdhouse is called a nesting shelf.

Some people think that phoebes bring good luck. Make several Phoebe Nesting Shelves. If a phoebe nests in your yard, maybe your luck will change for the better!

Level: 2

Tools Needed:	*Materials Needed:*
scissors	2-liter green plastic soda
marker	bottle
ruler	thumbtacks

1. Draw a line around the bottle, 6 inches below the cap.
2. Cut along the line. Discard the top half of the bottle.
3. Cut a rectangular piece out of the top edge of the remaining part of the bottle, 2 inches deep by 5 inches across.
4. Trim off the top corners at an angle.
5. With your scissors, make a couple of slits, ¼-inch long, in the bottom of the

bottle for drainage. These slits will keep rainwater from filling the shelf and flooding the nest. (The bottom of plastic bottles can be hard to cut. You might want to ask a parent or teacher to help you make the drainage holes.)

Best Place to Hang Your Shelf: Phoebes like to nest above doorways, but a doorway isn't usually the best place for a nesting shelf. People going in and out of the door—opening and closing it—will disturb nesting birds. Find a quiet place for your nesting shelf under an eave or porch. If possible, rest the shelf on a wooden beam. Secure it tightly to the beam with thumbtacks.

Best Way to Clean the Shelf: After the phoebes have finished raising their family, take down the nesting shelf and discard the old nest. Wash the shelf with warm, soapy water. Once dry, it's ready to go back outside. Don't be surprised if young phoebes from the first brood stay around your yard. They often do.

If you're lucky, phoebes will nest in the shelf you build for them.

Hollowed-Out Gourd House

Gourds are related to pumpkins, cucumbers, and squash. Many people grow gourds in their gardens. In fall, you can buy gourds at your local vegetable stand or grocery store. Some people use gourds as decorations. You can also use a gourd to make a birdhouse.

You won't be able to use your gourd birdhouse right away. Make the Hollowed-Out Gourd House in the fall and let it dry over the winter. In spring, when the birds arrive, your birdhouse will be ready.

Level: 3

Tools Needed:	*Materials Needed:*
serrated knife	a large, long-necked
teaspoon	gourd
felt-tipped marker	a few feet of wire or
scissors	string

1. Draw a 1½-inch-wide hole at the gourd's center.
2. Using a serrated knife, cut around the hole. (Have a parent or teacher help you.)
3. Put your teaspoon into the hole and scoop out the seeds and pulp inside the gourd. Getting all the pulp out might be hard. Do the best job you can.
4. Using the tip of your scissors, poke two small airholes, 2 inches from the top of the gourd.
5. Using your scissors again, make a hole through the neck

of the gourd, about the thickness of a pencil.

6. Thread wire or string through the hole and tie both ends together to make a loop for hanging the birdhouse.

7. Let the birdhouse dry indoors over the winter.

8. Hang the birdhouse in the spring.

Best Place to Hang the House: Hang your birdhouse from a tree limb or metal hook. Pick a spot in your yard that receives both sun and shade.

Best Way to Clean the House: After nesting season, take the old nest out of the house and wash the inside of the gourd house using a garden hose. Let the gourd dry completely before hanging it back up outside or storing it away for winter. Your gourd birdhouse should last for a few seasons if you store it in a cool, dry place during winter.

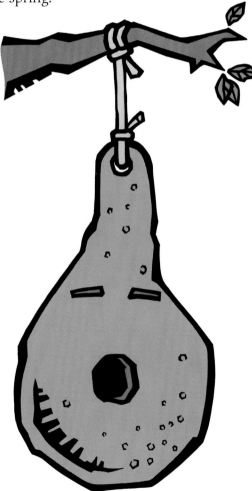

Variation: A house with a 1½-inch hole will most likely attract swallows. Changing the size of the hole will make the house attractive to other species. Make a house with a 1-inch hole to attract wrens or a 1¼-inch hole to attract chickadees (you'll need a smaller spoon to scoop the pulp through a smaller hole). Make several gourd houses with different sized holes and place them all around your yard.

Tree swallows will nest inside gourd birdhouses, decaying trees, and nesting boxes such as this one.

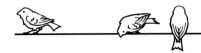

Natural Birdhouse

You can't go out and buy Natural Birdhouses. You have to go out and find them. Natural birdhouses are made by nature. They come from dead trees that have fallen to the forest floor. When you first look at them, dead trees don't seem to have much value. But they do. Dead trees provide nesting places for woodpeckers, chickadees, titmice, and other birds.

As trees decay, they often break apart into sections. A two-foot-long section makes a perfect Natural Birdhouse. Once you begin to look for Natural Birdhouses, you'll be surprised how many you find.

Level: 3

Tools Needed:
wire cutter
spoon or garden spade

Materials Needed:
section of decaying tree
 trunk
several feet of wire

1. Find a piece of decaying wood. (Look for a section with a little moss growing on the outside. The moss tells you that the wood inside is soft.)
2. Using a spoon or garden spade, make a hole in the middle of the wood. (Be careful not to dig through to the other side.) The hole should be about 1½ inches wide.
3. Reach into the hole with your fingers and remove the loose wood. You don't have to remove it all. The bird that uses your birdhouse will finish the job.

4. Cut two pieces of wire and wrap them tightly around the top and bottom of the log. The wire will keep the log from falling apart.
5. Use more wire to fasten the Natural Birdhouse to a tree.

Best Place to Hang the House: You can mount your Natural Birdhouse on a live tree in your yard. Wire won't hurt the tree. Find a partly sunny spot for your birdhouse and fasten it about four or five feet off the ground.

Best Way to Clean the House: Because it's made of decaying wood, your Natural Birdhouse will probably last only a season or two. But use your own judgment. If your Natural Birdhouse seems to be holding together, keep using it.

After nesting season, remove your Natural Birdhouse from the tree and shake out whatever debris the old tenants have left behind. To help your birdhouse last longer, store it in a cool, dry place during winter.

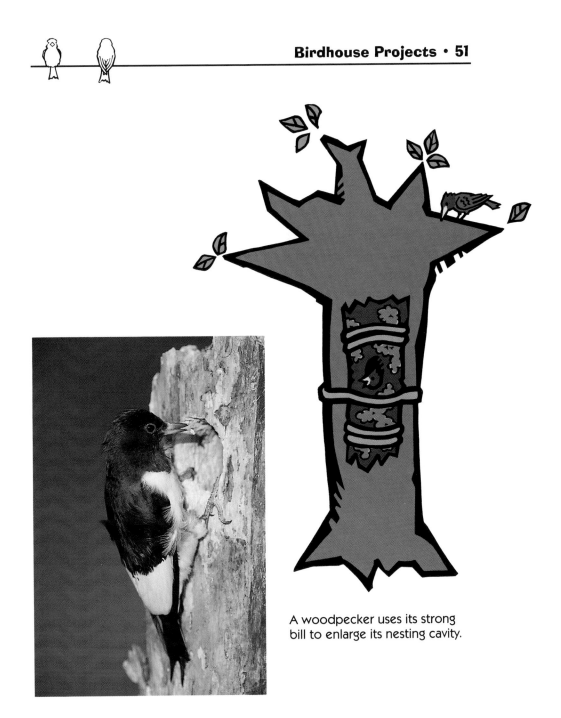

A woodpecker uses its strong bill to enlarge its nesting cavity.

GLOSSARY

binoculars: handheld optical devices that magnify, or enlarge, images. Binoculars help bird-watchers get a better view of faraway birds.

birds of prey: birds that get their food by hunting small animals

brood: a group of young birds that are hatched and cared for together

burrows: holes in the ground that animals use for shelter

camouflage: coloration or markings that help an animal blend in with its surroundings

cavity nesters: birds that build their nests inside protective structures such as burrows or decaying trees

clutch: a set of eggs that are incubated together

embryo: an animal in an early stage of development, before birth or hatching

fecal sac: a waste-filled sac produced by young birds of some species

field guide: A book that gives pictures and descriptions of different kinds of birds. Field guides help bird-watchers identify the birds they see.

fledgling: a young bird that has acquired the feathers needed for flight and is ready to leave or has just left the nest

incubation: keeping eggs in a nest warm enough for the chicks inside to develop and hatch

instinct: a natural ability or knowledge that an animal has from birth

migrate: to travel from one location to another, usually to reach new feeding or breeding grounds

nesting: the process of building a nest, laying eggs, and raising young birds

non-cavity nesters: birds that build their nests in open areas, not inside protective structures

ornithologist: a scientist who studies birds

predators: animals that hunt and kill other animals for food

species: a specific kind of animal within a larger group of similar animals

A herring gull chick

A black-necked stilt with eggs

Index

About the Author

Dean T. Spaulding is an environmental journalist and wildlife photographer. His work has appeared in *Audubon, Wild Bird, Birder's World,* and other publications. He is a member and former president of the Adirondack High Peaks Audubon Society and lives in upstate New York.

John Monroe

For more information:
National Audubon Society
700 Broadway
New York, NY 10003
212-979-3000